NOETIC PRAYER

AS THE BASIS OF MISSION
AND THE STRUGGLE AGAINST HERESY

Archimandrite Ephraim Triandaphillopoulos

NOETIC PRAYER
AS THE BASIS OF MISSION AND THE STRUGGLE AGAINST HERESY

Archimandrite Ephraim Triandaphillopoulos

Preacher of the Holy Diocese of Sisanium and Siatista, Greece

Translated by Gregory Heers
Edited by Moses Hawk and Fr. Peter Heers

Uncut Mountain Press

NOETIC PRAYER AS THE BASIS OF MISSON AND
THE STRUGGLE AGAINST HERESY

uncutmountainpress.com

Cover Artwork by George Weis.

Scriptural quotations are primarily taken from the King James
Version. The translator has emended some quotations to better
reflect the original Greek text.

Library of Congress Cataloging-in-Publication Data

Noetic Prayer as the Basis of Mission and the Struggle Against
Heresy—1st ed.

Written by Archimandrite Ephraim Triandaphillopoulos
Translated by Gregory Heers
Edited by Moses Hawk and Fr. Peter Heers

ISBN: 978-1-63941-008-8

I. Eastern Orthodox Christian Theology
II. Eastern Orthodox Christian Spirituality

The present work
is dedicated to my revered mother
Despina G. Triandaphillopoulos

Table of Contents

St. Paul the Apostle

PREFACE

In this present work, appealing to the blessings and prayers of His Eminence Metropolitan Anthony, and despite our spiritual shortcomings, we shall try to prove, by studying heresy and heretics in view of the soul and spirit, that unceasing prayer is a necessary provision in our struggle against heresies—in collaboration with the material and technological means our age offers, of course. The Orthodox Church is fundamentally ascetic. A well-established and sure conclusion of our age-old tradition is that the spiritual work inside us, this mystical labor, comprises the best work within our neighbor, the image of God, and thus within any heretic, atheist, person of another religion, etc.

The word of God, through the mouth of St. Paul, says "for there must also be heresies among you, that they which are approved may be made manifest among you,"[1] inspiring us in our encounter with heresy, to undergo a trial of faith and experience, but also to enter into unspeakable spiritual joy and gladness upon receiving those who return.

---

1   I Cor. 11:19.

St. Joseph the Hesychast

CHAPTER I
Heresy as a Spiritual Disorder

In his renowned epistles, Elder Joseph the Cave Dweller vividly describes for us the process by which delusions and heresies are born. In particular, he writes the following in Epistle Thirty-Six:

Take, for example, a spring by the seashore that wells up clean water. Suddenly a storm breaks out, the sea rises, and our little spring is polluted with sea water. No matter how clever you are, you will not be able to separate the sea water from the spring's water. The same thing happens with the nous.

The demons are spirits. Therefore, they are akin to and can be assimilated with our spirit, the nous. The nous is the purveyor of the soul, for it brings every appearance and perception of a noetic movement to the heart, which in turn filters it and gives it to the intellect. Therefore, the nous can be deceived just as the spring was polluted in the example. That is, the unclean spirit stealthily pollutes the nous, which in turn, as usual, gives whatever it has to the heart. If the heart is not pure, it gives the murk to the mind, and then the soul is darkened and blackened, constantly accepting fantasies henceforth instead of theorias. In this manner, all the delusions arose and all the heresies occurred.[2]

---

2   St. Joseph the Hesychast, *Monastic Wisdom: The Letters of Elder Joseph the Hesychast* (Florence, AZ: St. Anthony's Greek Orthodox Monastery, 1998), pp. 187-188.

Once the mind falls into delusion, it is very hard for it to return; the devil has a powerful grip on it. The delusion of the mind is terrible and difficult to understand. At another point, Elder Joseph emphasizes:

For when someone gripped by delusion obeys someone else, it is possible for him to be delivered from it, and for the evil one to lose control of him. This is why the devil advises and persuades him not to believe anyone anymore and never to obey anyone, but henceforth to accept only his own thoughts and trust only in his own discernment. Lurking within this haughty attitude is that huge ego, the Luciferian pride of the heretics and of all who are deluded and do not want to return to the truth.[3]

It is very hard, if not impossible, for the atheist, the heretic or for any deluded man to come to an understanding of his condition, which presupposes repentance. It is hard for him to believe that he is in error, that what he believes does not represent the truth but falsehood. On the contrary, the sinner always has the chance to be saved. One modern-day elder had the following opinion:

If we had on one side a thousand deluded people and on the other a thousand extremely sinful people, nine hundred ninety-nine of the sinners would be saved, except for one unrepentant person; while of the deluded, the issue is whether one would change. And this is because a deluded man does not change easily. Delusion is a sweet pill. The sinner may be saved with one "I have sinned" as the thief on the cross. But with a deluded man things are very difficult. He is gravely ill, as one with advanced leukemia; it is conceit, in fact, a feeling of being different than others.

---

3   Ibid., 189.

Even the thirst for learning which distinguishes them (i.e. heretics) is adulterated. All the virtues are contaminated: humility with acting humble, silence with acting the part of an ascetic, love with fleshly desires, prayer with showing off, tears become an end in themselves, faith with heresy, etc.

Their thirst of knowledge is morphed into pleasure derived from reading, a pleasure which has to do with "being someone special." This pleasure passes into the body, which is wholly shaken in a whirlpool of self-love. One is intoxicated with knowledge. This pleasure is a spiritual passion, which takes over the soul entirely, affecting the body as well. Thus, having taken the intoxication of knowledge as theological revelation, the Gospel and Patristic texts are misinterpreted.

Many of those who delight in reading the beautiful and highly theological writings in Holy Scripture and the commentary of the Fathers understand them and have their fill of them, so to speak. But unfortunately afterward, having grown too bold and familiar with them, they treat them as if they were their own creations. This spiritual familiarization of them with the mind, which is already darkened by the passions of vainglory and conceit, begets the fruits of cacodoxy, delusion, wickedness, and heresy. This is somewhat how the great heresiarchs and all the heretics fell.[4]

Deficiency or excess in the means of the spiritual struggle may lead to heresy. Deficiencies and excesses are the evils that must be avoided. In the erecting of the soul's spiritual structure, moderation in everything is the royal way. One must also be careful with respect to the imagination.

---

4   Notes of an elder with the title, *Counsels of a Spiritual Father*, unpublished, 221 [in Greek].

Usually the imagination is divided into four sub-groups: (1) that which has to do with the promotion of the passions of every kind, (2) that of musing or daydreaming, (3) that of artists and cultural creators, and (4) the most dangerous, theological imagination or that of theological creation. This last kind thrusts the praying Christian into the pit of heresy and delusion. "Raw knowledge is united with the rational intellect through the imagination, giving birth to theological apparitions, offspring of delusion, of theosophy, and children of pride."[5]

We continue:

The heart must first be cleansed and then it can become the abode of the Holy Spirit, that is, when pride and delusion are uprooted. Long before this, however, when the intellect is still blinded by the passions and desires to pray noetically, that is when it begins to believe somehow that it feels God's consolation. This, of course, is [within the realm of] the imagination and not the senses. If we rely on our imagination, it will form whatever images it desires, even of the Lord Himself, the Theotokos, the saints, paradise, etc.

This is where the descent of the so-called enlightened ones begins, who are all deluded, as they believe they supposedly venerate the angels, our Lord, the Holy Trinity, the Holy Spirit and so much else.

They even go further, giving their own arbitrary interpretations and creating unfortunate circumstances in the Church.

When excessive gladness and stillness of the intellect exist through humility, a lack of restraint leads the inexperienced to vanity, the attempt to please others and a sick sentimentalism regarding spiritual matters. According to the experience of the neptic Fathers, in all spiritual matters, even with respect to the divine energies of the uncreated Light of the Trinity, when

---

5   Protopresbyter Anagnostopoulos Stephanos, *Ανασασμοί Σωτηρίας* [*Breaths of Salvation*], Piraeus, 1999, 568 [in Greek].

Divine Grace contracts there lurks the ever-present threat of hidden demonic attacks of vanity.[6] "Let him that thinketh he standeth, take heed lest he fall."[7]

The heretics forget that which the Fathers, who theologize because they know God, continuously call to mind: to stand as babes, continually with humility, as beginners and forever students of Grace. And this is given to them as a perpetual, well-grounded feeling and internal acknowledgment.

Elder Joseph writes: "For example, you say, 'I am a sinner!' But deep down, you consider yourself to be righteous. You are unable to avoid delusion. Grace wants to remain, but since you haven't really found the truth yet, necessarily it has to leave. For without a doubt you will come to believe in your thoughts that say that you are something you are not. Consequently, grace does not stay."[8]

Likewise, the unquenchable thirst for spiritual knowledge and lofty spiritual matters leads to undesirable circumstances. Again, as Elder Joseph writes: "If you ask for grand things before their time, the Lord does not give them to you, because He gives things in due order. But if you keep burdening Him with your requests, He allows the spirit of delusion to imitate grace and deceive you by showing you nonsense. Therefore, it is not beneficial to ask inordinately."[9]

Likewise, the incorrect confession of deeds, but mostly of hidden thoughts, may lead to a serious problem. Hidden thoughts, pushed back into the depths of the heart, are reinforced, and "as they operate secretly and imperceptibly, they mature further,"[10] notes Saint Neilos of Ancyra.

---

6   Anagnostopoulos Stephanos, 14.
7   I Cor. 10:12.
8   St. Joseph the Hesychast, *Monastic Wisdom*, Ninth Letter, 75.
9   St. Joseph the Hesychast, *Monastic Wisdom*, Tenth Letter, 81.
10 Ascetic Homily, St. Neilos, Ch. 48. See: Ιω. Κορναράκη [John Kornarakis], Αναφορά στα Θέματα Ποιμαντικής Ψυχολογίας [*On Issues Related to*

In conclusion, we will touch on the second part of the present study saying that a serious and collected man makes sure to stay aware of the conflicts of his soul. He is reconciled with the unpleasant and disagreeable experiences of life, "so that he not collect repressions in the depths of the unconscious part of his personality which will disturb his soul's equilibrium."[11]

Professor Kornarakis writes: "Through repression, a person believes that he has nothing to do with it, yet his unconscious is occupied with confronting the problem, without the person knowing how his unconscious operates. Therefore, repression does not rid us of the (psychological) problem. On the contrary, it entangles us in an affair that is not unfolding under the light of the consciousness but within the darkness of the unconscious."[12]

The divine ladder of St. John leading to heaven

the treasure of a miser

all devouring Hades

He who has united his heart to prayer will not easily be raided by spiritual thieves

Pastoral Psychology], εκδ.Κυριακίδη, Θεσσαλονίκη, [Kyriakides Press, Thessaloniki], 1991, 97.

11 Ιω. Κορναράκη [John Kornarakis], *Ψυχολογία και πνευματική ζωή* [*Psychology and Spiritual Life*], εκδ. Κυριακίδη, Θεσσαλονίκη, [Kyriakides Press, Thessaloniki], 1980, 29.

12 Ibid., 28-29.

CHAPTER II

Heresy as a Disorder of the Soul

Every heresy may constitute a disorder for the soul of the one suffering from it, while every psychological illness, even when it has religious content, does not constitute heresy, nor does it necessarily lead to it.

Heretics are those who consciously deviate from the healthy faith and reject one or more of the dogmas of the Church, persisting in their errors, even after the Church's counsel and admonishment in order to avert their fall.[13]

There is, therefore, a conscious creation of teaching and persistence in it.

We arrive at many important conclusions by studying the life of well-known heretics, such as Manetus[14] (AD 240, Babylon), Arius[15] (AD 230 Alexandria), Macedonius[16] (4th cent. AD), Nestorius[17] (5th cent. AD), Julian the Apostate[18] (AD 331-363), Origen[19] (2nd - 3rd cent. AD), Eutyches[20] (5th cent.), the Manichean Julia,[21] who troubled Saint Porphyry, bishop of

---

13 Θρησκευτικής και Ηθικής Εγκυκλοπαίδειας [Religious and Ethical Encyclopedia] (ΘΗΕ) vol. 1, Μαρτίνος [Martinos], 1089.
14 ΘΗΕ τομ. 8, 573-77
15 ΘΗΕ τομ. 3, 92-4
16 ΘΗΕ τομ. 8, 503-5
17 ΘΗΕ τομ. 9, 427-434
18 ΘΗΕ τομ. 6, 950-55
19 ΘΗΕ τομ. 12, 572-92
20 ΘΗΕ τομ. 5, 1106-9
21 Μάρκου διακόνου [Mark the Deacon], Βίος Πορφυρίου Γάζης [Life of St. Porphyrios of Gaza] (85, 4-6/13-19).

Gaza and missionary from Thessalonica (347-420), but also contemporary cases.

The Devil often takes advantage of spiritual gaps and psychological injuries, even a person's temperament, to throw them into delusion and heresy, in which we can detect from one's mental aspect, signs of hysterical neurosis, paranoia and even schizophrenia.

The heresiarch Manes, for example, inherited his so-called visionary idiosyncrasy from his father. He had two visions, in which he was informed that he was set apart from others and the time had come for his mission to begin. He believed these things to have been sent by the Comforter.

Heredity can play a role in the appearance of hysteric symptoms. There is a strong connection between hysteria and the particular structure of one's personality, just as intense visual and audio subjection also plays a role. These individuals have the desire and ability to be deceived. They are incapable of self-awareness and grasping reality in general. What is dangerous about the entire matter is that all these things are done consciously.

One's inner tendency to become the center of attention or the recourse to hypocrisy for personal gain is characteristic of all deviating forms of behavior, especially those related to hysteria.

Egotism is the root of hypocrisy. Not fulfilling the Christian ideal in our life, instead of humbling us, leads our will and the imagination to the creation of false ideals, according to which our life is directed, in the presence of God and our neighbor. We perceive such a life, which is actually false, as reality, as it appears to be true.

We observe the following in the lives of known heretics: first, tendencies of rebellion and conflict with local bishops; compulsive persistence in delusion, demonstrated in letters as well; an unusual zeal and unconventional methods of spreading heresy (e.g. Arius); the creation of factions; the concealing and disguise of their actual mindset, in the form of a game of hypocrisy. Arrogance, contentiousness, and fanaticism are the basis of external piety and virtuous ethics—at times to a pathological extent. Ambition accompanies slandering the bishop, who is often violently removed. Ascension to the throne takes place even under the curses of the Orthodox people (see Macedonius). Servile help is sought from courtier factors on the basis of the principle "to always accommodate those in power."[22] Oftentimes, the faithful undergo cruel massacres, and this is why the heretics are condemned as "the cause of many murders."[23] On other occasions, exceptional bodily and spiritual merits, such as an imposing presence, a booming voice, eloquence, and the like (e.g. Nestorius) give fuel to manic behavior against those they consider heretics. Nestorius' hostility, hatred and fanaticism even towards heretics seemed to be a "clinical example" and troubled the faithful, who called him a firebrand regarding the matter and suspected him of having a problematic way of life. They are called by the Church to make their defense, and they deny many times. A childhood in an environment full of harassment and persecution piles up repressed inclinations for revenge, precisely because the correct spiritual guidance is missing (e.g. Julian the Apostate). In other instances, we notice an intense curiosity for delving deeper into the meanings of texts, extreme forms of behavior, extensive learning, an unquenchable thirst for knowledge, writing and a strange divergent teaching, indicative of large internal conflict (e.g. Origen). All these things do not obstruct the appearance of an externally upright ethos. Persistence in fallacious beliefs leads even to the calling of a "robber" synod by means of violence and terrorizing (e.g. Eutyches, AD 449).

---

22 Σωκρ. Εκκλ. Ιστ. [Socrates, *Ecclesiastical History*], 4,20 [3,25].
23 Ibid. 2.42.

These elements and this behavior also characterize modern heretics. We will, however, focus our attention on other factors which clearly incline toward the pathological, with respect to both ancient and modern heretics.

Professor Stavros Baloyiannis writes: people who suffer from hysterical neurosis and possess a pathological religious sentiment maintain that they have a prophetic aptitude, or that they communicate with the saints, whom they see in their sleep or while awake and receive commands from them... and through these assertions they attract other people prone to such things, by whom they are designated as an object of reverence and worship. Usually the content of their teaching is superficial with an eschatological tinge, yet when they address theological issues, they often become agents of cacodoxy and heresies. They use speech that is strange and incomprehensible, shifting to a state of stupefaction. They write figuratively or draw incoherent things without speaking. The Gnostic heresy in the first years of Christianity is an obvious example of the dramatic turn and extent that the effects of projected mentally pathological elements can have within the context of religious sentiment.[24]

St. Paul's stance on the aforementioned matter is characteristic, as it expresses the unparalleled ability of discernment of psychiatrically pathological elements and the analysis of them: "I besought thee ... that thou mightest charge some that they teach no other doctrine, neither give heed to fables and endless genealogies, which promote questions rather than godly edifying in the faith, so do! Now the aim of the commandment is charity out of a pure heart, with good conscience and with faith unfeigned from which some have swerved and have turned aside unto vain

---

24 Σταύρου Μπαλογιάννη [Stavros Baloyiannis], Ποιμαντική Ψυχολογία [Pastoral Psychology], (Thessaloniki: Pournara Press 1980), 246, 248-49.

jangling, desiring to be teachers of the law, understanding neither what they say nor whereof they affirm."[25]

In the life of Saint Porphyry of Gaza (+420), during the incident with the Manichean from Antioch, Julia, who, "undermining the faith with her magical teachings, and much more with the money she gave (i.e. to the faithful)"[26]—calling to mind the tactic of modern Jehovah's witnesses—there is reference to the external appearance and behavior of her and her companions, which indicates also their spiritual disorder:

a) "the faces of them all were pale"[27]

b) "And they all did build their reasoning upon the teaching of this world, and much more Julia than the others. And their guise was lowly and their manner gentle, but, as it is said, they were outwardly sheep, [Matt. 7:15] and inwardly ravening wolves and venomous beasts; for hypocrisy is in all their words and deeds."[28]

Similar are the findings of Saint Gregory the Theologian on the external appearance and behavior of Julian the Apostate. During his encounter with his old classmate, he was not slow in realizing the delusion from up close, speaking, indeed, of madness.[29]

In the case of Julian, in particular, we will mention that he was initiated into the mysteries of the Sun King in a cave with lightning, illuminations, the summoning of spirits and magical acts. He believed that the Sun King chose him to save the kingdom from its enemies, chiefly Christians. He may have been initiated into the Eleusinian mysteries. He performed

25 I Tim. 1:3-7.
26 Βίος Πορφυρίου Γάζης [Life of Porphyrios of Gaza], 85, 4-6.
27 Ibid. 88:3.
28 Ibid. 88:4-8.
29 Παπαδοπούλου Στυλιανού, Ο πληγωμένος αετός: Γρηγόριος ο Θεολόγος [The Wounded Eagle, Gregory the Theologian], εκδ. Αποστολική Διακονία [Publications of Apostoliki Diakonia].

auguries, theurgies, magical rituals, reminding one of modern-day fanatic neo-pagans. He had also believed in the words of Maximus of Ephesus, a neo-platonic philosopher and theurgist, that he is the incarnation of Alexander the Great. At the hour of his death, he rebuked those crying around him because they were lamenting an emperor who was being united with the stars and the sky.[30]

One can easily recognize the pathological character in these things. Julian's seemingly logical and ambitious delirium, owing to his wide and disorderly education, cannot hide his underlying paranoia from an experienced eye.

Professor Baloyiannis writes: "One patient named John was wrapped in layers of leather straps and claimed to be St. John the Forerunner."[31] Elsewhere he writes: "Another patient, a scientist, confessed very intently and in parables to his relatives and friends on the phone that he was the Son of God, who came into the world for the salvation of his country. One week later he went on to confess the aforementioned opinions in public, in an amphitheater, calling all there to follow him in his salvific work."[32] These passages are found in his chapter examining schizophrenia.

Conditions just as serious appear in some of the faithful today, mainly victims of arrogance, incorrect spiritual guidance, and perhaps some idiosyncrasy as well.

One elder relates the following:

Someone came to confession and said: "I have no need of confession. You, priest, need to confess to me." "Why?" I asked. "Because I am a higher-ranking priest than you," he said. "And how do you rank higher?" The man answered, "I was ordained directly by St. Basil, and you by some

---

30 ΘHE vol. 6, 950 etc.
31 Ibid., 111.
32 Ibid., 112.

Metropolitan." "And St. Basil came down from heaven and ordained you? Ah, so the devil ordained you. Because no one is ordained by either angels or saints from heaven, but only by the hands of a bishop. Bishops lay their hands on other bishops, presbyters and deacons."

He was one of the "enlightened ones." Soon after he was admitted into a psychiatric hospital.[33]

In this case, the delirium that led him to psychiatric confinement was accompanied by his delusions of grandeur and heretical elements.

At other times, the faithful fall victim to deluded people:

"Three months ago, some children—eight of them, between the ages of 13 and 14—got together at a house, supposedly to play and to watch TV. One of them was pressuring and trying to persuade the others. There at the house they conducted a spiritual experiment, a séance… One of those children got the others to sit around in a circle. They held hands, lit candles, shut the windows and put one of the boys to lie down in the middle of the circle. The boy who invited them over played the medium, the mediator. They called the "spirit" of his dead grandfather in the name of the devil. They squeezed their hands, and the boy in the middle levitated into the air. One of the children opened his eyes because he felt a cold draft over him, and then because of what he saw he shouted, "Oh, my Christ! Mother of God! Help!" His parents were Christian, faithful members of the Church. The parents of the first boy often held séances in the house.

Then there was a loud noise. Everything in the room broke. There was smoke and a fowl stench. And the boy who had been lifted into the air fell down with a bang. From

---

33 Anagnostopoulos Stephanos, Protopresbyter, *Η προσευχή του Ιησού* [*The Prayer of Jesus*], p. 14.

his fright he couldn't speak. Three days ago, while under the stole of a spiritual father that boy was still mute; he was unable to speak. All the other children involved were suffering from a nervous breakdown, except for the one who called out for help from Christ and the Mother of God."[34]

Our comment on the matter is that which the deluded or heretical person has in him, he transmits when he finds fertile ground.

As for the "calmness" which is noted in the behavior of heretics and of which we will discuss later, what the ever-memorable Father Epiphanios Theodoropoulos says is both quite enlightening and clever: "In the villages, my child, when the villagers want to tie their donkey to pasture, they don't have to tie it up by all four. It's enough to tie it up by one leg. The Devil does the same with the Evangelicals. Since he has them tied by the leg of heresy, he doesn't attack them with other temptations. That is why they feel 'peace,' as they claim. This peace is artificial and fleeting."[35]

34 Ibid., 52-53.
35 Θεοδωρόπουλου π. Επιφανίου [Fr. Epiphanios Theodoropoulos],
    Υποθήκες ζωής [Counsels for Life], Ησυχαστήριον Κεχαριτωμένης,
    Τροιζήνα, 1992, [Troezene, Hesychasterion Kecharitomene, 1992,
    98].

CHAPTER III

Noetic Prayer as Restoration for Soul and Spirit

The world in which we live gives us the illusion of fulfillment, and that's why many people abandon God for the idols, new materialistic theories, eastern religions, delusion, heresy, etc.

Our nous, heart, and attention ought to become one through prayer, as Christ said, "two or three gathered together in My name."[36]

The Fathers encourage us to pray unceasingly—even if we do it orally—in the name of Jesus. They advise us not to be grieved that our nous is disrupted, not to despair, but on the contrary to rejoice that we bring it back to the words of prayer (St. John of Sinai).

The prayer that is said orally will draw the nous to attention and in time, through continual effort, it will cease to be distracted.

It is a given that the attempt is to be made in combination with a pure—as much as possible in the world within which we live—purging of our thoughts and deeds to a spiritual father, with the keeping of God's commandments and the practicing of virtues. In addition, the participation in the mysteries of our Church is considered absolutely necessary.

If we lack paying attention, in time it will become obvious to us that we labor in vain as regards prayer. At the same time, we will see through experience that prayer and attentiveness are united "like twin brothers" as the Fathers distinctively say.

---

36 Mt. 18:20.

Assuming these prerequisites, prayer in the Lord's name is all-powerful and fully effective; it incinerates and cleanses all uncleanliness. Whosoever has an attentive heart does not run the danger of demonic delusion. As God's Name descends into the depths of the heart, it humbles "the serpent that has held the powers of the heart captive, saving us and enlivening us."[37]

Prayer itself crushes pride and pays off our spiritual bankruptcy. And showing us the dragon within, this very prayer burns it up, and on another level, it heals the wounds that it inflicted.

With this internal undertaking the dirty thoughts are dried up, one's thinking is refined, joy is poured into the heart, harlotry is dried out, rage is driven off, grief is taken away, insolence removed and depression disappears.

"What we are to expect from prayer is the feeling of calm and warmth towards God settling in our heart. Enthusiasm and the pursuit of lofty meanings and principles are to be avoided[38]... [and one must be] on watch for self-satisfaction, self-regard, thinking highly of oneself, being proud of oneself, one's supposed superiority over others and any such mindset."[39]

This passage touches on two points, or aspects of egotism, to which the heretics did not attend: the theological imagination with the supposedly high conceptions and their high opinion of themselves. Trust in any apparitions, extreme egotism and ascesis while concurrently in mental prayer are fraught with insanity or heresy. On the other hand, humility attracts the spiritual dew.

Spiritual fathers and writers advise: "If you feel that your nous has united with your heart and you are no longer divided

---

37 *Νοερά Ἄθλησις* [*Noetic Exercise*], εκδ. Συνοδείας ΚΛΗΜΕΝΤΟΣ ΜΟΝΑΧΟΥ, Ἁγ. Ὄρος [Publications of the Brotherhood of Clement Monk, Mt. Athos], 1980, 71.

38 Ibid., 102.

39 Ibid., 142.

with sin,… you are united as though a whole… safeguard this God-given gift."[40]

Here it is implied that divine energy touches the crushed parts of the soul and heals them, unites them into one. In this manner, prayer drives out sorrow and grief, for from prayer springs such consolation, the like of which nothing else in this world can offer.

However, vigilance is necessary because vanity and various attacks from the passions approach the heart even now, regardless as to whether they are repelled, provided that at the entrance of the heart "attention stands as an unsleeping guard, which drives back enemies in the name of Jesus."[41]

More specifically Saint Theophan the Recluse writes: "again there are times when the enemy comes as a thief, managing to infuse a sinful, 'heavenly' sweetness, which is then immediately perceived by one watchful and expelled, and through repentance the heart is cleansed of any injected trace of filth."[42]

Progress in the spiritual life is reversely proportional to pride. Knowledge of "our personal unsuitability in all the meaning of the word"[43] must increase inside us constantly.

Athletes of this ritual exist not only in the desert, but in cities also. Though not a monk, His All-holiness Patriarch Photios, having taken upon the administration of the giant jurisdiction of Constantinople, was taught noetic prayer and had progressed to such a level that, according to St Symeon of Thessalonica, his person shone from the grace of the All-Holy Spirit, "as of a second Moses."

---

40 [*Noetic Exercise*], 343.
41 Ἐπισκόπου Θεοφάνους [Bishop Theofanes], *Ἅπαντα ἀλληλογραφίας* [*The Complete Correspondence*], vol. 4, No 705, 342.
42 Ἐπισκόπου Θεοφάνους [Bishop Theofanes], 342.
43 Ἐπισκόπου Θεοφάνους [Bishop Theofanes], 351.

This is because grace does not watch the external conditions and the magnitude of our passions as much as it does our own violence against them, and on account of this it works out the outcome of the temptations and our spiritual path.

The name of Jesus acts as a medicine whose operation remains unknown to us, but which can be seen by the results it brings about.

Indeed, the struggle against the passions sounds easy, but the change it brings to those struggling is often dramatic. Dreadful is "the blazing noetic dragon's reaction to the prayer cried out noetically,"[44] the learned monk, Theoklitos Dionysiatis, points out.

According to another work, it takes "streams of tears, with pain of soul until death, with utter humility, and with great patience. Blood must flow from over-exhaustion in saying the prayer. You have to collapse from exhaustion for weeks as if gravely ill. And you must not give up the fight, until the demons are beaten and withdraw."[45]

But also "when the passions are severed from the heart with the supranatural force of the prayer of the heart, then only the memory of them (i.e. the passions) remains in one's intellect, and if prayer and the fear of God become absent in man, then they are revived and renewed."[46]

It is emphasized here again that the lack of attention undermines the spiritual struggle.

The passions and the demons act on the wayside, on the confines of the heart. The grace of the Holy Spirit is in its depths.

---

44 Διάλογοι στον Άθω [Discources in Athos], εκδ. ΑΣΤΗΡ, β΄ εκδ. 1983 [ASTIR Publications, 2nd edition, 1983] p. 71.

45 St. Joseph, Monastic Wisdom, Third Letter, 51.

46 Νηπτική θεωρία [Neptic Theory], εκδ. Ι.Μ.Οσ. Ξενοφώντος, Άγ. Όρος [Publications of the Holy Monastery of Xenofontos, Mt.Athos], εκδ. ΟΡΘΟΔΟΞΟΣ ΚΥΨΕΛΗ Θεσ/νίκη [Publications of Orthodox Kypseli, Thessaloniki], 1991, 28.

The more a soul forces itself to pray, the more the evil spirit reacts, but at the same time the ability to fight it off increases.

Continuing: "after the prayer of Jesus reaches Satan's dwelling, the heart, and it rends and shakes it greatly, he himself is agitated directly and confused... just as hornets are agitated when someone strikes their nest. Put all your strength into the prayer of the heart in order to rend that veil of Satan."[47]

Such a vocabulary surprises us. The demonic struggle, the jousting with the evil one, is related vividly. We are admonished to "resist till death". We read:

"...either I will die at this moment from the excessive force of the prayer or the devil will be banished and abandon my heart along with his guile."[48]

This particular prayer is called a "noetic sword,"[49] of which "the wretched and coward was afraid."[50]

The terminology that follows reminds us of blood-letting or the opening up of an abscess by a doctor: "you call out for and invite the all-good doctor to enter into your words so as to heal your incurable passions... incurable because no one other than Christ is able to heal them... for the heart to be leavened with His comforting... Name... a need to employ a medical suction cup in this heart, which will take out and clean out the puss and the harmful blood from your heart, which has been wounded noetically and pummeled by the merciless noetic thieves... and in this way the prayer of the heart will latch on even more tightly within your chest and will remove from it all the lewd and evil thoughts and will cleanse it."[51]

---

47   *Νηπτική Θεωρία* [*Neptic Theory*], 75.
48   Ibid. 75.
49   Ibid. 78.
50   Ibid. 78.
51   Ibid., 128, 129, 132.

We feel as if we are in an operating room. First comes the operation, and then the cleansing.

In the first stage of the prayer there is some danger. The relative calm of the nous which follows ascesis in this prayer might be taken by the faithful for purity of heart. This is a delusion. The energy of the nous is in the brain, its substance in the heart. The intellect is easily cleansed and easily defiled, while the heart is defiled with difficulty and is cleansed with even more difficulty.

Saint Ignatius Brianchaninov writes, in particular, concerning the depths of action of mental prayer: "In the beginning, prayer leads the nous to a state of peacefulness and attentiveness. Later it enters into the heart and revives it, bearing feelings of repentance and compassion within it. More deeply, it begins to operate in all the parts of the soul and body and everywhere chase sin away, destroying the rule, influence and poison of the demons. Then there arrives unspeakable contrition and inexpressible pain of soul. The soul suffers like a sick person or a woman in labor. ("For the word of God is quick, and powerful, and sharper than any two-edged sword."[52])[53]

The way is difficult, but it leads to the royal chambers of our Lord Jesus. We read: "When the noetic prayer becomes active in the heart through Divine Grace, after toil, labor and much pain, the nous becomes clean, so bright and so open that it rises to the incomprehensible heights of theoria (vision) of God, yet always remaining in the Holy Spirit. Nevertheless, it takes discernment regarding delusions, perversities and all those false circumstances and false visions of the so-called enlightened.

---

52 Hebrews 4:12.

53 Ιγν. Μπριαντσιανίνωφ [Ign. Brianchaninov], *Υἱέ μου, δός μοι…* [*My Son, give to me…*], εκδ. ΟΡΘ. ΠΝΕΥΜ. ΚΕΝΤΡΟΥ ΛΕΜΕΣΟΥ [Publications of Orhodox Spiritual Centre of Lemesos], β' εκδ. Αθήνα [2nd edition, Athens],1989, 108.

Thus is man filled with infinite spiritual gifts. He is bathed in grace and his nous is now receptive to spiritual theoria, so that, enraptured, he wonders which of the visions (theorías) to choose."[54]

So having subjected and dispersed the enemies with the name of Jesus, and after a painful course of purification, the nous enters into the choir of the blessed spirits and goes into the formerly closed temple of the heart to offer true worship.

The Holy Spirit, which till that time had been calling and urging him only towards mourning and repentance, now calls on him to rejoice.

By enduring the fever of the passions, man proceeds from purification to illumination and finally to theosis (deification). He receives the equivalent grace respective to these three stages: purification, illumination, and perfection.

Elder Joseph the Cave Dweller describes these three stages very vividly: "The grace of 'praxis' is likened to the radiance of the stars; whereas the grace of illumination is like the full moon; but the perfecting grace of theoria is like the midday sun traversing over the horizon."[55]

Catharsis, or purification, means we fight with the passions. Illumination means clearness of the nous and depth of meanings. The things stand according to their nature, naturally in their actual truth. There is peace of thoughts and rest from temptations. Finally, enlightenment is followed by the third stage: pause from prayer, frequent visions, 'seizing' of the nous, cessation of the senses, immobility and utmost silence of the body's members, union of God and man inside bright light.

---

54 Anagnostopoulos, Stephanos, Protopresbyter, *Αναστασμοί Σωτηρίας* [*Breaths of Salvation*], Piraeus, 1999, 198.
55 Elder Joseph, *Monastic Wisdom*, Thirty-fifth Letter, 182.

SAINT GREG-ORY OF St-NAI

St. Gregory of Sinai

Icon from the workshop of Saint Gregory of Sinai Monastery (Kelseyville, CA).

CHAPTER IV

Heresy and the Worldly Spirit is Contrary to Noetic Prayer

Many times, aside from heretics and the deluded, even educated laymen and clerics position themselves against this prayer. Monks with good intentions, but who live a life of externals and do not comprehend the meaning of the interior life, are offended by the spiritual workers. They consider their behavior strange. They slander them, insult them and persecute them in various ways.

St. Seraphim of Sarov says: "People who are attached to what is outward and sensible oppose our heart's most cherished convictions with their opinions and do all they can to divert us from living an interior life."[56]

When St. Gregory of Sinai in the 14th century reached Athos and started to share his God-given knowledge with pious ascetics who were eager and intelligent, but understood service to God in only a bodily way, they opposed him at first.

Bishop Ignatius Brianchaninov states:

Still stranger does spiritual activity seem to the carnal and natural mind, especially when it is infected with the blight of conceit and the poison of heresy. Then the hatred of the human spirit which has entered into alliance with Satan against the Spirit of God expresses itself with unnatural fury. The carnal and natural mind distorts everything spiritual

---

56 Ιγν. Μπριαντσιανίνωφ [Ign. Brianchaninov], 2000.

in order to conform it with the darkness of the fall in which it gropes, despite its earthly learning.[57]

In the 14th century, Barlaam from Calabria reached Thessalonica. There, aiming to act on behalf of the Latins, under an Orthodox mantle (cf. modern-day Uniates), he renounced Catholicism. Having composed various works, to prove that he supposedly had the rectitude of the Easterners, he won the trust of the Emperor Kantakouzenos. Comprehending that monasticism was the support of the Church, he wished to weaken it and even to crush it, so that the whole Church might be shaken. So he expressed the wish to live a most austere monastic life and deceitfully persuaded a certain Athonite monk to reveal to him the skillful exercise of the Jesus Prayer.

Having gotten what he wanted, but having understood that the monk had revealed it to him in a strange and thoughtless way, he mistook the bodily aids (holding of breath, posture of body, etc.) for the essence of the matter.

A council was called at Constantinople (i.e. the Councils of 1341, 1347, and 1351). St. Gregory Palamas, an Athonite monk and great ascetic and practitioner of noetic prayer (who proposed that the oral exercise of the prayer start for children in school), entered into conversation with Barlaam and the latter's blasphemies were eventually anathematized. Barlaam returned to Calabria and Catholicism. Many Greeks, however, being flippant Christians, believed his teaching and brought it to the West, where his blasphemies and absurd slander were received as a confession of truth.

"Bergier, author of Dictionnaire Théologique, under the term hesychasm-hesychast (ησυχασμός-ησυχαστές) says that the Greek monks went mad trying to reach theoria, fixing their eyes

---

57 Ibid., 201.

on their belly buttons and holding their breath, imagining that they were seeing a bright light."[58]

The light which our Fathers speak of is not material, but spiritual, life-giving, joy-giving, uncreated, shining white, divine. It illumines the mind, opens the eyes of the soul and is seen by them, albeit it acts also on the material eyes, as happened in the case of the holy Apostle Paul.[59]

"It is a substantial shining of the power of the Holy Spirit in the soul, Through this light all knowledge is revealed and God is truly known by the worthy and beloved soul,"[60] St. Macarius the Great explains with clarity.

One modern-day elder explains:

The thoughts are burnt by the blinding hypostatic light which dissipates and dissolves anything that rises before it. There is only light. The mountain within the light vanishes and the shadow before this light disappears. Of course, when some saint prays, the first thing he feels clearly in his nous is the natural (created) light of his nous, and then if God wants, he comes into the vision of the Lord's light. How is the created light distinguished from the uncreated light? God comes to his aid and provides a special spiritual theoria with discernment.[61]

Of course, the Latins with their known theology of created grace have lost the key of access to these spiritual treasures, the essence of our faith which is summarized by, "I believe in the Lord because I see Him." As the Apostle wrote, "Even as they

---

58 Ibid., 209.
59 Acts 9.
60 Μακάριος ο μέγας [Macarius the Great]. 7, 23 in Ign. Brianchaninov, 205.
61 Anagnostopoulos, Stephanos, 562.

delivered them unto us, which from the beginning were
eyewitnesses, and ministers of the word."[62]

Paisius Velichkovsky, who lived towards the end of the 18th
century, in one of his treatises, refuted the blasphemies of some
philosopher monk with an earthly mindset, who lived in the
Moshiensky Mountains and was a contemporary of his. "Since
some monks," notes St. Ignatius, "who had a zeal for this prayer,
fell into delusion due to their pride or to their inexperienced
spiritual guides, they criticized the treatise and blasphemed it.
With the urging of the devil, this monk attacked the treatise to
such a degree that he went much further than the heretics
Barlaam and Akindynos. Some Christians of ill volition were
led to such madness by the philosopher's wretched words that
they drowned adherents [of St. Paisius' teaching] in a river,
tying them to a large brick. Unsatisfied with his blasphemies
being taught orally, the monk thought to publish them. However,
he was struck with the rod of God and became blind. Thus his
campaigns of opposition came to an end.[63]

He who is rich in earthly wisdom, a carnal and natural nous,
always looks at noetic prayer with much suspicion and dislike.
This prayer, as a means of union with God, is very abhorrent
and peculiar to those who take a liking to the company of fallen
and rejected spirits, which give them their own wisdom as if it
were something very great. Such a mind, such a soul and heart,
will find foolishness in noetic prayer, because it seeks wisdom with
the passions. "For the preaching of the cross is to them that perish
foolishness; but unto us which are saved it is the power of God."[64]

True Christians, however, in the seemingly impotent and
unimportant work of noetic prayer, find "Christ the power of
God, and the wisdom of God. Because the foolishness of God

---

62   Luke 1:2.
63   Ign. Brianchaninov, 206, 207.
64   I Cor. 1:18.

is wiser than men; and the weakness of God is stronger than men."[65] Contemporary people who are educated according to the world, who have no clue about noetic prayer in the Orthodox tradition, repeat the blasphemies of the Westerners, which is no surprise to us.

Modern-day Greeks who are worshippers of antiquity state that "it is not difficult to understand the role of Christianity in the birth... of other mental disorders.... Christianity teaches young people... that sexuality is a sin, or to be exact, that the understandable increased interest during puberty in the reproductive function is a sin per se and even that the human body and its functions are disgraceful. Those living a Christian life cause certified and wide-ranging forms of hysteria."[66] Elsewhere abstinence and a celibate life are called "hysteric anaphrodisia."[67] Let us imagine then how they would respond if they read the "Hymns of Divine Love" by St. Symeon the New Theologian. It is certain that the hysteria which they would fall into would exemplify all that of which they accuse us. And because they accept Freud's opinion that every monotheistic religion constitutes a total obsessive-compulsive disorder, they find a way out of the multiplicity of their passions ("legion") in ancient polytheism. And they call mental prayer a "continual obsessive repetition."[68]

All these "enlightened" people consider the frequent offering of the same prayer as something fruitless and meaningless, call it mechanical and say it consumes no energy of thought,

---

65   I Cor. 1:24-25.
66   Περιοδικό ΠΑΝΘΕΟ ΕΛΛΗΝΙΚΟ [Journal PANTHEO HELLENIC], vol. 11, χειμερινή τροπή [Winter] 2000, 89-91.
67   Ibid.
68   Journal PANTHEO HELLENIC, 89-91, τευχ. 11, χειμερινή τροπή 2000, σελ. 89-91.

appropriate perhaps for simple people. "Unfortunately, 'they do not know the secret which is revealed as a result of this mechanical exercise. They do not know how this frequent service of the lips imperceptibly becomes a genuine appeal of the heart, how man becomes immersed in the interior life, how the prayer becomes a delight, becomes, as it were, natural to the soul, bringing it light and nourishment and leading it to union with God.'[69] Those poor people forget that "except ye be converted, and become as little children, ye shall not enter into the kingdom of heaven."[70]

This prayer which we practice and they say is "mechanical and consumes no energy of thought" does not mean the oblivion of the nous as it happens to the Buddhists and those practicing yoga. The nous is set to continually appeal for divine mercy, in the depths of the heart. Simplicity, guilelessness of heart and refinement of the nous, to wit, go together to the glory of God and love of one's fellow man. Life continues as well, with its trials, adversities, and sorrows. Along with these things unceasing prayer exists, far from the fear of obligations that characterizes the exoticness of the supporters of eastern religions. The fire of prayer penetrates everything. Thus, the spiritual person is in all things in the world, but he himself is "not of this world." Though he judges all, he is judged by no one, as the Scriptures say (1 Cor. 2:15).

Simplicity of heart reminds us of the "harmless as doves,"[71] while the refinement and sharpness of our mind refers to "wise as serpents."[72] This is the golden combination of the great spiritual giants in Orthodoxy.

---

69   *The Way of the Pilgrim*, 23 (depending on edition).
70   Mt. 18:3.
71   Mt. 10:16.
72   Mt. 10:16.

CHAPTER V
The Missionary Method of the Fathers

"If a man is a heretic, after the first and second admonition reject him, knowing that such as he is subverted and sinneth, being condemned by himself."[73] From St. Paul's letter to Titus we have an example of how to confront heretics. Caution, however, is necessary, for if mission does not go hand in hand with the mystic work, then it is certain that instead of showing hate towards heresy, we are showing hate towards heretics; and we call this state of hatred "missionary estrus (heat)." This is a delusion.

Worthy of our notice in the life of St Porphyry of Gaza, written by Mark the Deacon, is the following phrase (referring to the saint): "having all his passions dead, save only that indignation which he stirred up against the enemies of the faith."[74] This means the use of anger as a natural nerve of the soul, provided that the mortification of the passions has come first.

That which ought to distinguish the shepherd from the heretics is the virtue of patience. The saint was not harsh and unrelenting against the enemies of the faith, except when he had patiently used all other means. When he came to know of the arrival of the Manichean Julia and that she had misled some of the newly illumined, he called her in order to learn whence she had come and what she believed. He didn't become angry

---

73 Titus 3:10-11.
74 *Βίος Πορφυρίου Γάζης* [*Life of Porfyrios of Gaza*], 28.

when he learned, even though those around him were agitated. (It is we who agitate and fanaticize those around us.) On the contrary, with much patience he advised her "both once and twice, keeping the word of the apostle."[75] He called her "sister," and when she challenged him publicly to converse, even saying "either you persuade me or I you,"[76] he accepted in all seriousness. We take note of this: he fasted and prayed much that the Devil be shamed.[77] On the following day, when Julia arrived with her company, he took the Holy Gospel and crossed his mouth with it. Only when the conversation dragged on for many hours and the blasphemies of Manicheans against God were heard and the saint was told "from above" that Julia was ruled over by the devil, did he say to her: "God, who made all things… Who is glorified in Trinity, shall smite thy tongue and muzzle thy mouth, that thou may not speak evil things."[78] And then "for Julia began to tremble and her countenance to be changed, and continuing as in a trance… but was voiceless and motionless… And after she had been for a certain time without speech, she gave up the ghost, departing unto the darkness which she honoured, holding it to be light."[79]

So his anger was not passionate and his zeal was thoughtful and according to knowledge. So let us not thoughtlessly differentiate against heretics and those of other religions, showing thus that we lack in experience and are of an impure heart. If we do act in this way, no matter how much the contemporary material-technological and information infrastructure may free our hands, we rather aid the establishment of heretical sects rather than struggle against them.

---

75   Ibid., 120.
76   Ibid., 120.
77   Ibid., 87.13.
78   Ibid., 89.7, 124.
79   Ibid., 90.2-11.

Let us look at the example of St. John of Kronstadt:
"He would usually ask those of other religions about their needs and their difficulties, without bringing up religious topics... he would receive representatives from the Jews who would thank him for a gift of his to the Jewish community... with his prayer he healed a Tatar, asking his wife: 'do you believe in God?' After receiving an affirmative answer, he said, 'we will both pray, you in your way and me in mine.'"[80] Was his Orthodoxy perhaps endangered? It is very likely that the healing of the Tatar led him to Orthodoxy as well. We see also the saint receiving a petition for a check of 20,000 francs from a French bishop, in order to purchase a orphanage from atheists, and the French ship captain, Zervé, to thank him for some precious gift and to ask him to pray for France."[81]

In a similar way Saint Philothei and Saint Arsenius the Cappadocian helped indiscriminately all those who were in need and ran to them, even those of other religions. Who can censure them for their pure Orthodox mindset? Fanaticism is alien to the children of God, while it eloquently points out our own illness.

However, when Saint Arsenius the Cappadocian's spiritual fold was endangered by heretical Protestants, teachers in particular (he was a teacher himself), his reaction was quick and direct: "Leave here quickly, as you are with your things, before you unload, because we do not want another Protestant in Farasa. The one we have is enough."[82] And in church: "whoever

---

Άγιος Ιωάννης της Κρονστάνδης [*St. John of Kronstadt*], σελ, 297, εκδ. ΠΑΡΑΚΛΗΤΟΣ, Ωρωπός 1994.

81 Ibid., 298.

82 Όσιος Αρσένιος ο Καππαδόκης [*St Arsenios of Cappadocia*], εκδ. Ησυχ. Αγ. Ιω. Θεολόγου, Σουρωτή [Publications of the Holy Monastery of St. John Theologian, Souroti], 39.

says good day to Koupsi, he should know that his remains will
not see decay."[83] And Fr. Paisius continues: "that was the only
answer, in order to isolate the hornet, Koupsi... and that's how
the hornets' nest of the Protestants was destroyed."[84]

The teacher and the shepherd ought to be diverse: continually
praying, full of life experiences. Beyond whatever knowledge
he has, being informed and being familiar with the potentialities
of modern tactics, it is his own experiences that will lead him
in the proper confrontation of the heresies.

It is mentioned in the life of St. Nicholas of Myra that "he
had so much grace upon him, such brightness and radiance of
love, peace and joy, that whoever looked upon his face became
well! And if they were a heretic, they returned to Orthodoxy!"[85]

Without experience we cannot direct people correctly, neither
can we persuade them. The well-disposed are drawn, from
wherever they may be, even from idolatry. The following is also
mentioned by Fr. Ananias Kustenes: "Until Heraclius brought
the Holy Cross from Persia, the Holy Cross did missionary work
there. St. Anastasius the Persian (January 22) was a child of the
Holy Cross. The Persians would go and see the Cross and those
who were well intentioned would go again. The Holy Cross
attracted them and without realizing it they gave themselves
over to it."[86] In other words, due to a lack of missionaries, God
was acting as a missionary, as though we men were not absolutely
necessary everywhere. And it is possible, sometimes unaware,
for us to obstruct His work. But as long as we live and are called,
let us stand humble and true.

---

83 Ibid, 40.
84 Ibid, 40.
85 Αρχιμ. Ανανία Κουστένη [Archimandrite Ananias Koustenis], *Λόγοι
    Α´* [HOMLIES 1], εκδ. ΑΡΜΟΣ [ARMOS PRESS], 1999, 18-19.
86 Archimandrite Ananias Koustenis, 18-19.

Zealotism and ecumenism are the two extremes which must be avoided. The second of the two is the most dangerous. The first one is visible. The second might co-exist with a spirit of "love," in the name of the universality of Orthodoxy, etc. The boundless use of rationalism likewise corrupts the genuine Orthodox spirit: Let us allow Elder Paisius who is full of life, to teach us:

Some out of kindness say, Don't say to the heretics that they are in error so as to show them "love." And thus they raze everything. If they were alive during the early years of Christianity, we wouldn't even have one saint. They used to say to Christians then, "Just put a little incense on the fire and don't deny Christ!" They wouldn't accept. "Just act like you're throwing it on!" They wouldn't accept. "Don't talk about Christ and you're free to go somewhere else!" They wouldn't accept. Today, you see a watered down world."[87]

And concerning rationalism, he says:

Unfortunately, Western rationalism has had an influence… we find ourselves in the Orthodox Church only with our body… they see the West ruling in a worldly way… if they could see spiritually, they would see… that it is gradually drifting into darkness… they gather to discuss matters… which are not up for discussion… the same person who neglects spiritual work has the idea that he is a spiritual person and then he talks nonsense… his mind, constantly spinning, is far from God, and thus he makes it a two-edged sword, slowly killing himself and cutting up others, as well… the mind alone is an iron cane, without a magnet, that hits

---

87 Γέροντας Παΐσιος [Elder Paisius], *Πνευματική Αφύπνιση* [*Spiritual Awakeness*], vol. 2, εκδ. Ησυχ. Αγ. Θεολόγου ΣΟΥΡΩΤΗΣ, [Publications of the Holy Monastery of St.John Theologian, Souroti], 1999, 46.

against metal objects so as to stick, but they just twist but don't stick... In prohibiting relationships with heretics the holy Fathers knew what they were doing.[88] Today they say, "Prayer with everyone, not just the heretics. The European spirit believes spiritual issues can fit into the Common Market, as well."[89]

Elsewhere, he says, "Can you mix gold and copper? Such a great struggle took place for dogma to be refined."[90]

Icon from Athonite (athoniteusa.com).

88 Γέροντας Παΐσιος [Elder Paisius], *Με Πόνο και αγάπη* [*With Love and Pain*] vol. 2, στις ίδιες εκδόσεις [the same publication as above], 210-211.
89 Ibid., 347-348.
90 Ibid.

CHAPTER VI
Modern-day Heretical Experiences

A more careful look inside us would show that we too as shepherds do not live our theology, which cannot be alien to what the Fathers have spoken, taught, wrote, and experienced. If I am one thing and my theology another, then I am living Nestorianism, a state that plagues and tortures the Church today, involving both clerics and laymen. We are referring to the well-known issue of the separation of dogma from ethos. It is as if we live the neutral union of Christ's two natures through simple contact. Although our Church confesses and declares the hypostatic union of the two natures of Christ unmixed, unchanged, undivided, and inseparable in the 3rd (431) and 4th (451) Ecumenical Councils in Ephesus and Chalcedon respectively, our life is as if it has not been entirely leavened with Christ's grace. Our confession of faith is something external, skin-deep. We commune Christ's Body and Blood and yet we continue to take the swine of the passions to pasture. The Lord, however, should envelop every aspect of our life, for, according to St. Gregory the Theologian, "that which is not assumed is not healed."[91] If we preach being as yet unhealed and devote ourselves to a struggle against heresy, we do not, in this instance, persuade our heretical brothers for whom Christ died.[92] They do not see the difference of the new creation in us. And rightly so they remain where they are. As for us, we do

---

91   PG 37,181 C.
92   I Cor. 8:11.

not escape the danger of transmitting "another gospel,"[93] different from that which we received, distorted and foreign. Our words are one thing, our life another. This is the incarnation of Nestorianism.

An example of this is the tendency which we have, both with the clergy and the laity, to divide areas into sacrilegious and sacred, even inherently so, as if we can exclude the existence of God from a sacrilegious area, or refuse to consider the act of unseemly behavior in a holy place as being spiritually unhealthy. The Lord, who is everywhere present and is present even in Hell, takes into account not so much the place as our behavior in the given place. And this behavior will either be holy or demonic. Instances from the lives of the saints and the sayings of the elders show the truth of this word.

This tendency, therefore, has a Nestorianizing hue, which agrees also with the dualism of the Manicheans and the Gnostics. Consequently, conversations are divided into spiritual and non-spiritual, even the members of the body are divided into honorable and dishonorable, as if Divine Grace did not touch the whole body at baptism or when the whole man is deified and the uncreated Triune Divine Grace touches the whole man, some body parts are left outside! Honorable or dishonorable are our thoughts and not our body members, which are very often united with the Divine Body and Blood. A careful reading of the Hymns of the Divine Love,[94] by perhaps the greatest mystic theologian in the Orthodox Church, Saint Symeon the New Theologian, would ground us appropriately. The man who is kneaded in both body and soul with the Grace of God stands before Him in all things and does not fear unholy members or sacrilegious areas. Such fixations show our own incomplete

---

93   Gal. 1:6.
94   Φιλοκαλια των Νηπτικων και Ασκητων, [Philokalia of the Neptic and Ascetic Fathers], vol. 19E, 19F, 1990, 1989.

purification and our own inadequate Orthodox experience. And, indeed, they are a mild neurotic reality aiming toward more intense struggle.

This distinction of honorable or dishonorable members, even in those rightly living their faith, but much more among those "preoccupation over the spiritual things," is a bit reminiscent of, to not say is indeed, a monophysitizing perversion. If some of the members of the body are unholy, why did the Lord assume a whole body and come bodily to associate with us? What does cognitive science's conclusion have to say to us? That there is nothing spiritual that is not simultaneously incarnate.[95] Bodily glorification is a lived reality. May the Platonic belittling of the body remain far from us, which the Latins inherited, with the result that their Christianity has ended up as a bodiless Christian ideology. The ideologies are nothing else but shades of truth demanding to be imposed as actual truths. The one real truth, however, is only Christ according to "I am the way and the truth and the life."[96] Whatever truths—even if they are religious ones—that are outside Christ are theological ghosts. And whatever religions there are in the world, they constitute neuroses (or even psychoses) from which only (rightly lived) Orthodoxy can free us, as the ever-memorable Fr. John Romanides would aptly say.

We mentioned before that the distinction of spiritual and worldly conversations is not correct from a spiritual point of view. What is important is the spiritual experience of the speaker. It is known that oftentimes dogmatically faultless homilies seem to us hollow and dull. That is because they are not lived. At other times, a simple description of the way a breadwinner

---

95 Π. Νικολ. Λουδοβίκου, Prot. Nicholas Ludwig, *Ψυχανάλυση και Ορθόδοξη Θεολογία* [*Psychoanalysis and the Orthodox Theology*], εκδ. ΑΡΜΟΣ [AR-MOS PRESS], 50, 2003.

96 John 14:6.

lives, making ends meet, fills us with heavenly comfort. The man of God experiences Christ, and for this reason whatever he may do, whatever he may say, is graceful and spiritually upright.

Again, the division of people as inside and outside the Church, when we persist to extreme degrees (we vs. you, etc.), may lead to the notion that we belong to a kind of club of "saved," "able," or even "elect," selected to save to others. And this is a type neurotic persistence with an element of grandiose thoughts about oneself, indicative of unsolved personal conflicts, which cannot hide their forced smiles, which transmit to us that false, "everything is alright, come with us." And let us now leave nor even speak of the scenario about "the chosen Greek people"... etc. The annual number of abortions alone is indicative of a people killing itself, and thus is everything but "chosen." As for our knowledge of the Patristic texts, our language, or the Orthodox Tradition, let us not comment on them either, even with regard to those "inside" the Church.

The relationship with one's spiritual father is also often shown to be problematic. Near a holy father, the children feel entirely free; they make spiritual progress; the relationship operates comfortably and is not confined; it is not ill at ease. And this feeling is present even if the father is not physically there. Unfortunately, here too, both spiritual fathers as well as spiritual children can go to extremes. Particular attention must be given to the intimate attachment to the person of the elder, which makes him into a kind of guru and for which he himself is responsible. How then would we [spiritual fathers] be in a position to talk about the delusion of guruism?

In our homilies, which many times are ineffective, we make the mistake of distinguishing the bad God of the Old Testament from the good God of the New Testament. This is another child of the dualism that we encounter. This tendency resembles Marcionism in the first few centuries of Christianity.

At other times, we threaten heretics with hell which awaits them, which is a sign of our spiritual inadequacy. The saint lives, or rather places himself beneath the entire universe, considering himself the worst of all.

St. Anthony the Great said that hell is "only for me, only for me."[97] If hell is only for me, not for the others (since they are all my superiors) how can I make it a subject for homilies and preaching? However, even when the Fathers touch on the possibility of our eternal damnation they do it with politeness, with nobleness, and they heal us.

All these problematic circumstances that characterize our life are smoothed out by noetic prayer in the name of Christ, combined, of course, with correct confession, having a spiritual father who is not under delusion, obedience to the teaching of Christ and our Church, and regular participation in the Holy Eucharist.

It will be necessary in the first place for us to put our own house in order, and then our heretic brothers will find peace beside us without any particular effort on our part, according to the known "it is more necessary to be cleansed than to cleanse, to acquire wisdom than to spread wisdom." Amen!

---

97   Paul Evdokimov, *L'amour fou de Dieu*, ed. Du Seuil, p. 34, 1973.

UNCUT MOUNTAIN PRESS TITLES

Books by Archpriest Peter Heers

Fr. Peter Heers, *The Ecclesiological Renovation of Vatican II: An Orthodox Examination of Rome's Ecumenical Theology Regarding Baptism and the Church*, 2015

Fr. Peter Heers, *The Missionary Origins of Modern Ecumenism: Milestones Leading up to 1920*, 2007

The Works of our Father Among the Saints, Nikodemos the Hagiorite

Vol. 1: *Exomologetarion: A Manual of Confession*

Vol. 2: *Concerning Frequent Communion of the Immaculate Mysteries of Christ*

Vol. 3: *Confession of Faith*

Other Available Titles

Elder Cleopa of Romania, *The Truth of our Faith, Vol. I: Discourses from Holy Scripture on the Tenants of Christian Orthodoxy*

Elder Cleopa of Romania, *The Truth of our Faith, Vol. II: Discourses from Holy Scripture on the Holy Mysteries*

Fr. John Romanides, *Patristic Theology: The University Lectures of Fr. John Romanides*

Demetrios Aslanidis and Monk Damascene Grigoriatis, *Apostle to Zaire: The Life and Legacy of Blessed Father Cosmas of Grigoriou*

Protopresbyter Anastasios Gotsopoulos, *On Common Prayer with the Heterodox According to the Canons of the Church*

Robert Spencer, *The Church and the Pope*

G. M. Davis, *Antichrist: The Fulfillment of Globalization*

Athonite Fathers of the 20th Century, Vol. I

St. Gregory Palamas, *Apodictic Treatises on the Procession of the Holy Spirit*

St. Hilarion Troitsky, *On the Dogma of the Church: An Historical Overview of the Sources of Ecclesiology*

Fr. Alexander Webster and Fr. Peter Heers, Editors, *Let No One Fear Death*

Subdeacon Nektarios Harrison, *Metropolitan Philaret of New York: Zealous Confessor for the Faith*

Elder George of Grigoriou, *Catholicism in the Light of Orthodoxy*

Select Forthcoming Titles

Nicholas Baldimtsis, *Life and Witness of St. Iakovos of Evia*

Georgio, *Errors of the Latins*

Fr. Peter Heers, *Going Deeper in the Spiritual Life*

Abbe Guette, *The Papacy*

Athonite Fathers of the 20th Century, Vol. II

This 2nd Edition of

NOETIC PRAYER
AS THE BASIS OF MISSION AND
THE STRUGGLE AGAINST HERESY

written by Archimandrite Ephraim Triandaphillopoulos
translated by Gregory Heers, edited by Moses Hawk and Fr.
Peter Heers, and a new cover design by George Weis, type-
set in Baskerville, printed in this two thousand and twenty
second year of our Lord's Holy Incarnation, is one of the
many fine titles available from Uncut Mountain Press, trans-
lators and publishers of Orthodox Christian theological
and spiritual literature. Find the book you are looking for at

uncutmountainpress.com

**GLORY BE TO GOD
FOR ALL THINGS**

AMEN.

Made in the USA
Columbia, SC
12 January 2025

50564600R00033